I0775964

The American Bison

Its Habits, Method of Capture and Economic Use In The North West

by Chas. Mair

with an introduction by Jackson Chambers

This work contains material that was originally published in 1891.

This publication is within the Public Domain.

*This edition is reprinted for educational purposes
and in accordance with all applicable Federal Laws.*

Introduction Copyright 2017 by Jackson Chambers

Self Reliance Books

Get more historic titles on animal and stock breeding, gardening and old fashioned skills by visiting us at:

http://selfreliancebooks.blogspot.com/

Introduction

I am pleased to present another book on the subject of the Buffalo or the American Bison.

The work is in the Public Domain and is re-printed here in accordance with Federal Laws.

As with all reprinted books of this age that are intended to perfectly reproduce the original edition, considerable pains and effort had to be undertaken to correct fading and sometimes outright damage to existing proofs of this title. At times, this task is quite monumental, requiring an almost total "rebuilding" of some pages from digital proofs of multiple copies. Despite this, imperfections still sometimes exist in the final proof and may detract from the visual appearance of the text.

I hope you enjoy reading this book as much as I enjoyed re-publishing and making it available to fanciers again.

With Regards,

Jackson Chambers

II.—*The American Bison—Its Habits, Methods of Capture and economic Use in the North-West, with Reference to its threatened Extinction and possible Preservation.*

By CHARLES MAIR.

(Read May 27, 1890.)

There is perhaps no fact in the natural history of America which brings such reproach on civilized man as the reckless and almost total destruction of the bison. Twenty years ago it abounded in many parts of the North-Western plains and prairies; to-day there are in all probability not five hundred animals alive on the continent. In the beginning of this century it roamed the country from Texas and New Mexico northward, and from the Alleghanies westward into and beyond the Rocky Mountains and north-westward to the affluents of the Mackenzie. In remoter times, if old writers and their references to the animal are trustworthy, its range seems to have been almost continental. Indeed, if Hakluyt is to be believed, he saw the bison three hundred years ago in Newfoundland. But as he saw it "far off," he probably confounded it with the caribou. Purchas got much curious information from the Indians who accompanied Pocahontas to England, and from others with regard to Virginia, and mentions in his "Pilgrims" that large animals resembling domestic cattle were seen by the early adventurers into that region. Virginia was a wide term in those days, and in the district beyond the Alleghanies, now known as West Virginia, there can be no doubt that in 1616 the bison was a common animal. But there is no proof that at that time it frequented the region east of the mountains. Similarly the statements of Thomas Morton, in the "New English Canaan," one of the earliest works descriptive of the settlement of New England, must be looked upon with distrust. In this curious book, published in Amsterdam in 1637, the author describes the bison, from hearsay, as abounding in great herds in the neighbourhood of Lake Champlain, and states that the Indians manufactured its wool into cloth. Elsewhere he argues that the Indians are descended from the dispersed Trojans, and believes in the existence of the "Wild Ankies," certain strange beasts which were supposed to haunt Massachusetts Bay. He had a liberal fancy, therefore, and must be looked upon as a doubtful authority. Such references as the foregoing have been seriously accepted by various writers as a proof that the bison has, at one time or another, ranged the whole sub-arctic continent. The historic evidence on the point is certainly insufficient; but with the knowledge we now possess of the habits of the thickwood buffalo, the assumption cannot be called absurd. It is true there is no mention of the bison in Florida, where it might reasonably be supposed to have abounded; and we are told that it was pointed out to Cortez, in the menagerie of Montezuma as a rare animal from the north, so that it cannot have been a native of Mexico at the time of the conquest. But it must be borne in mind that the great ruminants are erratic in their range, sometimes abandoning a particular region for many years, and for no apparent reason, and then suddenly returning to it. This is the case with the moose, which for almost half a century was unknown throughout the country north, east and west of Norway House, on Lake Winnipeg, but which now abounds in that region. Though historic evidence, then, does not sustain the theory of the continental range of the bison, neither does it establish a contrary theory, nor invalidate the opinion of authors of eminence that it must have been well known to the ancient Mexicans, and was in all probability their milch and draught animal. Unquestionably one of the first white men to meet the animal in its native haunts was Cabaça de Vaca, one of the four survivors of the daring expedition of Pamphilo de Narvaez in 1528. This adventure was subsequently rivalled by the romantic folly of Coronado, who set out from New Mexico in 1541 in search of the fabulous city of Quivera. The historic interest which surrounds these adventures partly redeems them from the cruel disposition and greed which underlaid them. The "golden city of Quivera," like the Appalache of Narvaez and De Soto's El Dorado, was a delusion, and Coronado might have perished in his quest but for the countless herds which he passed through, " seeing nothing," as his reporter says, " but skies and bison for miles together."

Mr. Parkman, in his " Pioneers of France," makes mention of a wood-cut of the bison, which appeared in the " Singularités" of André Thevet, published in 1558, and which was probably the first of its kind. Others, again, have attributed the earliest accurate picture to Father Hennepin, who, over a century later, gave a rough print of the bison in his "New Discovery." The former writer doubtless drew the animal from description, and the latter from observation ; and it is thus a question to whom the honour properly belongs. The famous and infamous Father, as everybody knows, was the first white man to ascend the Upper Mississippi ; but seven years previously Père Marquette and the trader Joliet had descended it from the mouth of the Wisconsin to the Illinois country, and it is to the latter priest that we are indebted for the first graphic description of the bison. He represents it as resembling our domestic cattle. "They are not longer," he says, " but almost as big again, and more corpulent. The head is very large, the forehead flat, and a foot and a half broad between the horns, which are exactly like our cattle, except that they are black and much larger. Under the neck there is a kind of large crop hanging down, and in the back a pretty high hump. The whole head, the neck and part of the shoulders, are covered with a great mane like a horse's, which is at least a foot long, and renders them hideous, and, falling over their eyes, prevents them seeing before them. The rest of the body is covered with a coarse, curly hair like the wool of our sheep but much stronger and thicker. It falls in summer, and the skin is then as soft as velvet. At this time the Indians employ the skins to make beautiful robes, which they paint with various colours."

With the adventure of Marquette and Joliet, the animal fairly entered into northwest history, and became thenceforward an increasingly important element in exploration, pioneer settlement and trade. The success of every expedition into the western wilderness more or less depended upon it ; and from the time that the brave and unfortunate La Salle met his death through a wretched squabble over some buffalo meat, unnumbered tragedies, with whites and savages for actors, have attended its chase down to recent days.

Since Père Marquette's narrative was written, the animal has been drawn and described so often that everyone is familiar with its form. By a common misnomer its relationship has been assigned to the buffalo of the old world. The identity of the Euro pean and American bison has been questioned by Cuvier and other naturalists, but there can be no doubt that they are closely related. The former frequents solely certain mountainous recesses, whilst the typical western animal, though by no means confined to them, is essentially a creature of the prairies. Remains of the ancient ure-ox of Europe seem to identify it with the American prairie bison; and, this being the case, we may infer that existing differences in structure are due to altered habitat brought about by that great enemy of wild nature, the white man. The physical differences consist mainly in the length of mane and leg, the American animal being more low-set than its European congener. But these differences are not greater than those which mark the animal's form and habit on this continent, if we can speak in the present tense of a race which has almost perished. During my long residence in the North-West I have had the opportunity of consulting many Indians and half-breeds of experience and of great repute in their day as plain hunters, and thus of pursuing inquiries into questions of interest, with regard to the bison on the safe ground of their daily contact with and intimate knowledge of its habits. Of course observation being a varying faculty, opinions did not always agree. Some men saw differences and made mental note of characteristics which were entirely unnoticed by others. Men, too, who were old twenty years ago, and whose memory ran back to days when the vast region west of the Mississippi was a howling wilderness, had a primitive knowledge not possessed by latter-day hunters. In those days the great buffalo herds roamed almost unmolested. The Indians of course lived upon them, but, with savage conservatism, severely punished anyone who wantonly butchered them. Left thus to follow their own instincts, not driven from place to place by merciless persecution, nor intermingled so as to blend all in indiscriminate hordes, the herds possessed a distinctive character, and seemed to have their roughly defined boundaries, like the Indians themselves. Even down to recent years the difference between the animals in size and general appearance—in a word in what may be called breed—was recognizable, and of course led to special nomenclature in the various Indian tongues. The southern or "Missouri cattle," as they were called by the plain hunters, varied in some degree from those of the Saskatchewan. They were long-backed and heavy, the full grown cow often dressing to five hundred pounds and over of clean meat. They were frequently seen north of the Missouri, and were readily identified by the practised eye of the plain hunter, not only by their muddy coats but by differences in form. The northern animal, called by the Crees Pusquawoo-moostoos, or "the prairie beast," was shorter in the back and was noted for its hardy constitution and fleetness. A third animal was known upon the plains as Amiskoo-sepe-moostoos, viz.: "the Beaver River" buffalo, for a reason I have never heard positively explained. There are two Beaver rivers in the North-West—one which joins the Assiniboine near Fort Ellice, and the other which falls into Lake Isle à la Crosse. The winter habitat of this variety of the buffalo in the last century may have been on one or other of those streams, and so have given a distinctive name to a remarkable breed. It was a diminutive animal compared with the ordinary prairie bison, and had a closely curled coat, and short, sharp horns which were small at the root and curiously turned up and bent backwards, not unlike a ram's, but quite unlike the bend of the horns of the ordinary bison. These animals were probably numerous at one time, but became rare, and were noted as the latest to go north in the fall. The thickwood buffalo again—the Sakawoo-moostoos of the Crees—differs strikingly from all the others, though some writers seem to think it the offspring of animals detached by accident from the great herds. If so its progenitors must have been isolated from their fellows at a remote period. The thickwood buffalo is said to be much larger than the prairie animal, to have longer and straighter horns, and a shaggier and darker coat, though I do not vouch for these particulars, having never seen either the living animal or its robe. Its range is now confined to one or two affluents of the Upper MacKenzie, but sixty years ago it was found at Shoal Lake, east of Lake Manitoba, and within recent times it roamed the forests north of the North Saskatchewan. Indeed it would not be astonishing if remains of this animal should be found north of the Great Lakes, though no traces of its presence there have ever been met with so far as I know. But as domestic cattle can subsist and work, even in winter, upon the browse of the spruce or pine, the wood buffalo may have had a much wider range in times past than we have any record of. Certain it is that the animal has acquired the browsing habit ; has lost all desire to migrate to the plains, and is now to all intents and purposes a moose in its instincts and habitat.

The hue of the bison's coat seems to be everywhere of uniform brown, deepening in some instances into black. But freaks in the matter of colour are not unknown. I have never heard of a brindled buffalo, but now and then animals were killed whose colour was white and others whose foreheads were marked with a single white star, and others with a patch of white upon the belly. These variations seem to point to admixture with domestic stock, and heredity is no doubt responsible for them, though its effects may be due to a remoter cause. The colour of the primitive wild cattle of England is white ; and the white beavers, minks, muskrats and even otters which are occasionally trapped in the North-West perhaps illustrate a tendency in nature to revert to original types.

The annual migration of the plain buffalo was at one time an interesting feature of its life and movement, and one upon which the welfare of whole communities largely depended. The buffalo hunt was the mainstay of the Red River settlement, and of many other remote and isolated communities, both in the United States and our own territories, down to the era of railway extension and development. To such its movements were of the last importance, and a failure the source of dismay and suffering. But the great migration in by-gone years seldom failed, and was of such a character that few tribes or outposts of civilization, from New Mexico to Peace River, were long sufferers for want of food. The great Texan, Missouri and Saskatchewan herds, when undisturbed, had their migratory range within tolerably well-known limits until remorseless pursuit and destruction confounded all habitudes and instincts in one general fear and indiscriminate flight. The direction of migration was not invariably up and down the continent, though this was the popular belief. I have heard Hallett and Gaddy and other noted half-breed leaders of the plain hunt in times past, speak of Red River bands whose migration was from east to west, and vice versa. There were small bands, too, which seemed to roam in all directions, and many solitary bulls, driven off from the main herds, were scattered here and there, which could scarcely be said to migrate at all. But the migration of the great Saskatchewan herd was undoubtedly from north to south in the spring, and conversely in summer and fall. It was possible in the latter season to check the animals for a time in their northward march. Their senses were very keen, and at that time their dread of man seemed to overpower their migratory instinct. Hence the Indians took great pains in the fall to conceal themselves, if they did not wish their onward march to

be interrupted.   But in spring nothing could stop the southward progress of the herd.
By night as well as day it swept onward in living torrents which no obstacles could turn
from their paths.   In crossing the two Saskatchewans precipitous banks were often the
scenes of frightful destruction, the rear hordes pushing the vanguard over with irresistible
force.   Myriads perished by falling through the rotten ice, and one old traveller mentions
having counted 8,000 animals mired at a single ford.   The spring migration began as soon
as the thaw set in.   The bulls and cows formed into files, the cows taking the lead, and
all went south, invariably following the old paths, multitudes of which are worn deep
into the prairie soil by centuries of use.   It was at this season and in the fall that these
paths which interest strangers so much were formed.   No one now-a-days takes the pains
to trace out these paths for any distance, but if one were to do so one would find that
they are astonishingly direct routes from point to point.   As a matter of fact they were often
made use of by the early adventurers.   La Salle and his nephew, Moranget, followed them
in the fatal wilds of Louisiana in 1687, and many a wanderer has since been led by them
to water and to safety in the bewildering deserts of the south and west.   When once
fairly out on the broad plains the buffaloes scattered, the cows keeping to themselves, and
all fed like domestic cattle.   Early in July the rutting season began and then a terrific
scene of roaring and running took place, including innumerable bull fights often of the
most deadly character.   The young bulls came off victorious, and often ended the contest
by burying their horns to the roots in their elder antagonists, though sometimes both
combatants perished.   Of course the noise caused by such a tumult and concourse of huge
animals, often numbering tens of thousands, was stupendous, and, incredible as the statement may seem, by putting the ear to a badger hole, could be distinctly heard at a distance
of thirty miles.   If one will endeavour to pronounce the monosyllable him-m-m-m with
closed lips and without break, one will have a good idea of the continuous sound of a
great buffalo herd conveyed by the earth as through a telephone wire.   After the fighting
ended intercourse began, and invariably took place in the act of running ; preceded,
however, by a fact in natural history so singular that were there not ample testimony to
its truth, I should hesitate to set it down.   The young and victorious bulls selected the
old cows, whilst the young cows became the property of the old bulls.   To this curious
custom may be traced, of course, the singular features of the buffalo dance which was
performed by all plain Indians just before or during the animals' rutting season.   This
dance, though to all seeming a sensual orgy, was in reality a serious ceremony akin to the
Andacwandet, or sickness-cure of the Hurons, though not as gross.   Both sexes joined in
it, the males wearing masks made of the head of the buffalo with horns attached, and
imitating throughout the dance the antics of the animal with remarkable fidelity.   At
its close the young warriors took the elderly women, and the old warriors the maids, and,
leading them to the door of their respective lodges, there left them.   It would appear
that individual attachments occasionally arose between the male and female buffalo ;
not commonly indeed, for intercourse, subject to the curious custom referred to,
was with them as with domestic cattle.   But I am satisfied that, if not pairing, something
remarkably like it occasionally took place.   In general, when attacked by hunters, the
herd ran in a compact body, the cows in the centre and the bulls around them.   In the
scurry and mêlée, the shooting of cows, which were the animals generally singled out for
slaughter, drew no attention from the bulls—all swept on and left them.   But instances

have been known of a cow falling, and of a bull remaining at her side, not through accident, but evidently from feeling. He would stay by her, lick her, try to lift her up with his horns, and fiercely charge anyone who ventured to approach, long after the chase was over. It is difficult to explain such a scene upon any other grounds than that of personal affection—a sexual altruism which would not be surprising if it were not in opposition to natural habit. On the broad plains, when feeding and desiring to drink, the whole band, as if seized by a common impulse, would gallop off in loose order, and seek water at the same time. When not grazing the favourite occupation of the animals was wallowing, a curious summer custom (for the bison did not wallow in winter) and which, from its frequency, seemed to have something of the nature of a sport, as well as a sanitary purpose. There are many great prairies on the Saskatchewan where these wallows literally touch each other in all directions. Thousands of animals engaged in the exercise at the same time, and seen at a distance, the dust raised by their writhing looked like pillars of smoke arising from innumerable fires. These wallows are some-times confounded by new-comers with the *têtes des femmes*, as they are called, or rough depressions and hummocks caused by fire penetrating and interlacing in the sod. Another kind of depression has been a still greater puzzle, not only to the chance traveller, but to the geologist. I refer to those circular hollows wrought deeply in the prairies, each of which has a solitary boulder generally in its centre. These excavations were undoubt-edly the work of the bison, and in fact might be called its "tool-chests." Up to its fourth year the animal did not frequent them, but after that age it began to polish and sharpen its horns, and used the big boulders literally as whetstones. The soil constantly scraped by the shuffling of countless hoofs around these stones, was caught up and swept off by the wind, and thus in time these great depressions were formed in the prairie which without a knowledge of one of the most curious habits of the bison would be a standing mystery.

As summer advanced the Saskatchewan herds moved north, and as winter came on left the prairie. The cows seemed to be the hardiest, and often fed in the open until intense cold set in, when they, too, sought the shelter of the woods. It is generally sup-posed that in winter they scraped away the snow with their hoofs to get at the grass, like the Indian pony ; but this was not the case. If the snow was crusted, or hard packed, they used their fore feet to break it down, and then with their noses cleared away the snow. When loose it was invariably shoved aside in this manner ; and hence the animal's head, up to the eyes, was often quite shorn of hair before spring. Domestic cattle have the same habit, and strayed animals have been known to winter in the deep snow region of the North Saskatchewan, and turn up in excellent order in the spring. Hardened by a strain of buffalo blood I believe they would easily carry themselves over the winter in that luxuriant grass country. It is quite unlikely that the plain Indians ever tried to reclaim the buffalo as they did the Spanish horse, when it became a wild animal. The latter exactly suited their needs, and enabled them to run down their prey, instead of capturing it by cunning, with the added and glorious excitement of the chase. The taming of the buffalo was unnecessary to them as a source of food in regions which abounded with it naturally, and before the introduction of the horse their simple effects were easily transported by dogs. If milk was required, a cow was sometimes killed, and the fluid taken from the udder. It was very nutritious, but not so rich as the milk of the hind, or female red deer, which is almost a pure cream, and is sometimes taken by the Indians in the same way. While touching on this point one can scarcely pass over the references in old books to "The White Indians," as they were called, a nation indefinitely placed by writers in the last century at some point on the Mississippi or the Missouri.

In the "Concise Account of North America," published by Major Rogers, in 1765, it is said: "These Indians live in large towns and have commodious houses; they raise corn, *tame the wild cows, and use both their milk and flesh.*" This is plainly a reference to the Mandans, a singular race which was almost exterminated by small-pox some fifty years ago, and which is probably now extinct. They were of a fairer complexion than the surrounding nations, from whom they differed greatly in manners and customs; and it was a common conjecture, at one time, that they were descendants of the immigrants who left Wales, and sailed westward with Madoc in the twelfth century, and were never heard of afterwards. The Mandans made pottery, and built boats which closely resembled the Welsh coracle. These are well-known facts, and the statements quoted from Rogers are also true, with the exception, perhaps, of the taming of the buffalo, which cannot be vouched for. Maize is called by the North-West half-breeds "Mandan corn" to this day. It was largely cultivated by this remarkable race, who built villages of large timber houses, partly excavated in the ground, wherein numbers of families lived, and in which they stabled their horses in emergencies, feeding them on the bark of cotton wood saplings, which they cut in lengths and used as fuel. Another hazardous conjecture has sometimes been made, that the Mandans were the degenerate remnants of the mound-builders, whose vast earthworks indicate an organized social condition, and could scarcely have been constructed without draught animals. More advanced intelligence, indeed a high degree of civilization must have existed, perhaps contemporarily with the mound-builders in ancient Mexico and Central America; and it is difficult to believe that such stupendous architecture as that of Mitla or Palenque was the result of man's unaided effort.

In the presence of such facts there is no absurdity in the supposition that the bison was once a tame animal, and no violation of probability in Bryant's vision of the mound-builders as a "disciplined and populous race." When the Greek was hewing the Pentelicus and rearing the Parthenon, it is not improbable that the mound-builders of the Ohio were "heaping with long toil the earth,"

" When haply by their stalls the bison lowed,
And bowed his manéd shoulder to the yoke."

The bison seems to have been free from the ordinary diseases of domestic cattle. Untrammelled life and wholesome food no doubt kept it in good condition. Yet it was subject to a complaint peculiar to itself, a kind of itch or mange, called by the plain Indians *Omikewin*. This disease was confined to the bulls, and appeared on them after the rutting season. But it had its analogue in great epidemics which, at long intervals, raged upon the plains, and destroyed thousands of buffaloes of all ages and both sexes. An animal afflicted with this disease presented a sorry spectacle. The coat became loose and fell off in large tufts, leaving the exposed skin scabbed and loathsome with sores. It was contagious, too, and careless hunters, by using saddle-cloths cut from diseased hides, often communicated it to their ponies. The contagion, which spread, and did such mischief to horses, all over the territories some twelve years ago, was believed at the time to have originated in this way. Like wild creatures generally, the bison was free from deformities. I have often been told, however, that androgynous animals were not infrequently killed in the chase, an assertion which is stoutly maintained by old plain-hunters who profess to have seen them. Others think the so-called hermaphrodites were simply animals which when calves had been emasculated by wolves, or, as was sometimes the case, by hunters in rude sport. These beasts, whatever they were, grew to an enormous size, and were called by the English and French half-breeds,. "The Burdash," a name which is probably Norman French, for it is not Indian. If I am not mistaken the word *Bredache* in the patois of the French Canadian peasant designates an animal of both genders. Its Cree name was Ayā-quāyu, meaning "of neither sex." Such an animal, with its colossal frame, its vast front, and spreading horns was a striking object in a great herd, and, when killed in season, yielded what was known as the "beaver robe." This robe was greatly prized for its immense size and glossy, silk-like coat, and sold, twenty years ago, for ten times the price of the best robe of commerce.

Reference was made at the beginning of this article to the abundance of buffaloes within recent times. According to the Hon. H. H. Sibley, of Minnesota, the last animals ever seen east of the Mississippi were killed by the Sioux at Trempe à l'Eau, in upper Wisconsin, in 1832. For many years afterwards they were still very numerous on the great western and north-western plains. In 1868 the late James McKay, the well-known Red River half-breed trader and hunter, told me that some ten years before he had travelled with ponies for twenty days through a continuous herd, and on all sides, as far as he could see, the prairies were black with animals. It was not in fact until the construction of the first Pacific railway that a serious inroad was made upon their numbers. Indeed, as Dr. Carver very truly says, "As the Indians hunted them the race would probably have lasted for ever." But the building of that railway, and the subsequent extension of the Northern Pacific line, rang the knell of the buffalo. Immense numbers, it is true, had been annually slaughtered in the great plain hunt of the Red River half-breeds ; a system which was organized early in this century, and continued in full force down to about 1869, after which it began to languish. Many of the hunters formed small settlements in the interior, and instead of returning to Red River, sold their robes, etc., to traders on the spot. In its palmy days the plain hunt annually attracted nearly half the population of Red River. Fully four thousand people, including men, women and children, and a thousand carts, went off in early summer to the plains, and when the great herds were reached, and the "runs" took place, as many as two thousand animals were often killed in a single day. No doubt this involved great waste ; but food and leather were the objects of the plain hunters, as well as robes, and, hence, their destruction bore but a small proportion to the immense slaughter, in recent years, by the American pot-and-hide hunters. These men, in order to gratify the cravings of wealthy citizens for tongues and humps, were formed into large parties, with lavish outfits supplied by eastern firms, and being within easy reach of the great herds by rail the work of extermination speedily began. In due time the pot-hunting gave way to hide-hunting, which was found to be more profitable, and then the havoc became truly stupendous. The hunters' weapons were of the best, and their method so systematic, that the very skinning was done by horse-power. The dead bison was fastened to a stake and the necessary incisions made, after which a span of horses was hitched to the hide, and off it came. The hides were shipped to the nearest railway points in waggons, and the carcasses were left to rot upon the ground. In this way it is estimated that in three years nearly six million animals were destroyed. " But no one," says Dr. Carver (who is responsible for the foregoing statements), " will ever know what immense numbers were killed by these hide-hunters." " At the close," he says, " of one winter a man could go along the banks of Frenchman River for fifty miles by simply jumping from one carcass to another. Considering facts of this kind it is not surprising that some small tame herds and a few old circus animals represent the great herds which less than a quarter of a century ago blackened miles of prairie as a thunder cloud darkens the sky."

In bygone days the Red River plain-hunt often led into the very heart of the Dahcotah country, and frequent conflicts took place in consequence between the half-breeds and the Sioux, in which the latter were often the gainers. Some fifty years ago the English half-breeds, headed by the celebrated William Gaddy, were suddenly attacked on Goose River in Dahcotah by some two thousand mounted Sioux. The half-breeds had encamped, and their horses were nearly all at large on the prairie. In this raid by dexterous tactics the Sioux contrived to band up the plain-hunter's horses before their eyes, and after a short skirmish made off with three hundred choice buffalo runners, a blow from which the English half-breeds did not recover for years. Good runners were valued very highly in those days, and fetched as much as £60 and even £80 sterling each.

But any extended reference to the oft-described Red River plain-hunt, its organization, rules and methods, does not enter into the scope of this article, in which I seek to place on record facts less generally known, and features and incidents which are illustrative rather than striking in themselves. The oddest feature of the plain-hunt was the variety of weapons it called into play ; and its most interesting incidents the presence of mind and quickness of perception exhibited by the hunters in emergencies. The most antiquated fire-arms, mended and re-mended for generations by the ingenious Indians, or Metis, until all identity with the originals was completely lost, figured in the scene in company in latter days with ancient pistols and modern revolvers, the Sharp, the Ballard and the Henry repeater. The lance, which was simply a scalping knife warped with sinew to the end of a pole, or the knife alone, was used at close quarters. But the favourite weapon, particularly of the plain Indian, was the bow and arrow. It did not drive the animals frantic like firearms, and was even more deadly and much safer. The bow was about four feet and a quarter long and was made of the osage orange in the south, but of the choke-cherry in the north, a wood which is as tough as English yew. It was wound along its entire length with sinew, and strung with the same, and when drawn by a strong man, has been known to drive the arrow clean through a buffalo and into another. The arrow was half the length of the bow, and was made from the saskatoon, or *poire*, a tall shrub which sends up straight and elastic shoots very suitable for the purpose, and which bears a purple berry once greatly used in making pemmican.

The Sioux arrow was triple-plumed for six inches up from the notch. The arrow head was a piece of hoop-iron like an elongated **V**, very sharp in point and edge, and warped to the shaft with sinew and Indian glue, made by boiling the sinew down. Three irregular grooves ran along the shaft from feather to head, each in line with a plume, to give rotary motion probably, to the shaft in flight, or as some think, to give outlet to blood, though this seems absurd to one who examines the grooves with any care. The quiver and bow-case were made either of buffalo leather or deer skin elaborately ornamented with quill or bead-work, or of dog-skin dressed with the hair out, and both cases were connected by a sling-strap ornamented, if possible, with otter fur, which was greatly valued by the plain Indians. When hunting the buffalo, aim was generally taken behind the shoulder or behind the ribs, where the arrow-head by the heaving of the animal's flanks soon cut to a vital part, if it did not penetrate it at the first, and brought it to the ground. The bow and arrow is still in use, and few things more surprised the eastern volunteers in the rebellion of '85 than to find a weapon employed against them which probably had hitherto been associated in their minds with Crecy or Robin-Hood.

Great nerve and readiness were frequently called for on the part of the buffalo hunter, and serious accidents often occurred in the chase. I have listened to many camp-fire stories in the North-West more sensational than the following ; yet the two or three which I give, though not very startling, are authentic, and the incidents may be taken as typical of situations which called for coolness and resource. In 1847 Atchamaganis, or " The Trader," left Fort Carlton for the Sandy Knolls to procure meat. He came to buffalo, and after a run drove an arrow into a huge bull. In the act of stooping to draw it out the animal suddenly turned, and The Trader's horse swerved, and threw him clean upon the bull's head, where probably he would have been gored to death but for the lucky chance of one of its horns passing under his belt. This prevented tossing, and there "The Trader" hung, whilst the terrified bull made off at full speed. The situation was enough to shatter ordinary nerves, but "The Trader" took things coolly, and gathering himself together in such a way as to get a purchase, severed his connection with the horn either by the breaking or the loosening of the belt, and so fell to the ground, whilst the bull, too frightened to reflect on things, sped on, and left "The Trader" unhurt. Pruden, another hunter, after a sharp run, got his horse in line with, but slightly to the rear, of a swift buffalo cow, which stumbled whilst he was in the act of drawing the bow, and fell directly across his path. Without an instant's hesitation he urged his horse to the leap, and, springing clean over the prostrate cow, turned and transfixed her with an arrow. Owing to the peculiar bend of the buffalo's horns it was unable to toss a man who lay flat on the ground, and many hunters have saved their lives by a knowledge of this fact, and by acting upon their knowledge on the instant. Massam, an Indian, was thrown in front of a bull by his horse stumbling in a badger hole. In this fall he was caught by the bull and tossed twice, and severely ript in the leg. The third time the bull missed him, whereupon he fell to the ground, and lay still, though suffering dreadful agony. It was not the bison's custom to trample his foe. It would get astride of him, and nose him, and paw up earth upon him, with its fore feet ; all of which this particular bull did to Massam, and then, having exhausted its rage, left him, Gardapui, another practised hunter, some twelve years ago was thrown in the snow, and endured for hours the baffled rage of a bull until some fellow-hunters came up and relieved him. These occurrences show what men could do in emergencies ; but, of course, the buffalo had also its triumphs, and frequently made away with its pursuer. A bull was once killed which had a human pelvis stuck fast on one of its horns—a strange laurel won in some solitary struggle. The bison, when disturbed, does not rise with the lumbering slowness of the domestic ox, but has the faculty of springing on all fours at once. There is also, sometimes, something very like shamming in its conduct, when brought to ground by a shot and apparently dead. In this condition it has been known to lie perfectly still until the hunter came close up to it, and then spring upon him, and impale him in an instant.

Very dangerous at times were certain sulky old bulls, which having been driven off from their herd, nourished, like some human beings, a hatred of everything living. Genereux, an old Hudson Bay man, in passing with a dog-train betwixt two thickets of timber, was suddenly pounced upon by one of these morose animals, which tossed dogs, sled and all into the air, and made a wreck of the outfit. Another, maddened by the persecution of some Indian dogs, charged a large train of carts numbering scores which was on its way from Battle River to Fort Carlton, loaded with pemmican and dried meat. The infuriated brute rushed among the oxen and ponies, smashed collars and shafts and injured almost every cart before the astonished freighters could collect their senses, and shoot it.

But the buffaloes never were so dangerous to man as their pursuers ever have been to each other. The history of the North-West plain Indians down to the time of the transfer of the territories was simply a history of raids and reprisals begot of the horse stealing which was begot of the chase. This does not closely concern my subject, but it may be fittingly recorded here that the last of the purely Indian fights in the territories took place between the Blackfeet and the Crees, twenty years ago, on the plains southwest of Batoche, on the South Saskatchewan. The lives lost in the fight were few, but the lives lost in consequence of it were many, and the struggle might almost be called the Saskatchewan bison's avenger. The dancing over a Blackfoot scalp taken in that fight, and which was infected with the virus of small-pox, spread that fatal disease all over the North Saskatchewan, and decimated the Cree race.

As the bison has practically passed away, so the economic uses to which it was put by the natives and early immigrants in the North-West have passed away with it. Most writers have made note of one or other of these economies and doubtless all of them have been described. But it is none the less in place to bring them together in a paper like this, since they are closely related to my main subject. As a food the flesh of the buffalo was inferior to domestic beef in nutritive qualities; but if less satiating it was much more digestible. The tongue, hump, back fat and marrow bones were the choicest parts of the animal. The tongues, taken in winter and cured in spring, were beyond all comparison delicious; much more delicate, indeed, than the domestic, or even the reindeer tongue, and not so cloying. To cure them they were steeped in cold, then in tepid water. Six quarts of common salt, with some salt-petre added, were rubbed by hand into a hundred fresh tongues, after which they were put into a vessel, weighted down with stones, and allowed to soak in the brine, thus formed, for fifteen days. They were then taken out and strung up in pairs upon poles in the ordinary lodge or cabin, and when dry-smoked were fit for use or export. For the latter purpose they were generally cured at the Hudson Bay Company's posts, and as many as four thousand were thus treated at Carlton in a single year.

The boss or hump, a curious protuberance upon the shoulders of the buffalo, had a separate set of ribs, inosculating with the spine, and consisted of alternate layers of exquisitely tender fat and lean meat. It was the most highly prized part of the animal, and in one of average size weighed about thirty lbs. The " back fat," which was rich, but less delicate, lay immediately beneath the hide, and ran along and over the back-bone. It was about two inches thick, but thinned towards the rump, and weighed about fifteen lbs. in an animal in good condition. Back-fat was very abundant in the buffalo, but is not found to any extent in the domestic ox. Marrow-fat was the plain Indian's butter, and surpassed it in richness if not in flavour. It was prepared by breaking all the bones, and boiling them in water till all their oil was extracted. This was skimmed off, boiled again and clarified, and then poured into buffalo bladders, where it hardened into a rich golden mass which looked exactly like well-made butter.

Dried meat was a staple food in the North-West, and was made from thighs and shoulders sliced circularly into large sheets, and dried on stages over slow fires, or in warm, clear weather, in the sun. It was then made up into bales and would not spoil unless exposed to the rain. Though a highly nourishing food it never seemed to satiate. In travelling it was actually munched between meals through sheer habit, akin to the gum chewing of the Americans. A story is told of a French half-breed guide who astonished a stranger by his performances in this way, and who, being asked by his amazed companion why he never ceased eating dried meat, replied: "Ah, Monsieur! c'est pour passer le temps!" (it is for pastime).

From the dried meat and tallow of the buffalo the famous pemmican was made, at once the most portable and sustaining of foods. Pemmican was the device of the plain Indians, and has been made by them from time immemorial. It is first mentioned in the narrative of Coronado's New Mexican expedition of 1541, and the last bag of it was probably eaten on the banks of the Saskatchewan in 1882. I mean, of course, the buffalo pemmican, for it has been made occasionally since by the half-breeds from domestic beef. A sack or "toreau" of pemmican, as it was called, consisted of nearly equal quantities of tallow and dried meat, the latter being pounded on bull hides with stone hammers, axe heads or flails. From the siftings of the dried meat the "fine pemmican" was made in which marrow-fat was used instead of tallow; and the "berry" pemmican, the most highly valued of all, consisted of these two and a due proportion of saskatoon berries, or of choke-cherries, if the other could not be had. The single toreau weighed about 100 lbs., a double sack being over twice that weight. In making it the pounded meat and fat were constantly stirred in a bull-hide trough till they "set," and the mixture was then run into bags made of buffalo hide, sewed with sinew, with the hair side out, and pounded down with a mallet till they were full and compact. The ends were then sewed up, and a sack of this food, when properly made and stored in a dry place, would keep for years. Its value as compared with fresh meat was in the ratio of four to one, eight pounds of the latter being the customary daily ration, which was all eaten, whilst two pounds of pemmican were sufficient.

The buffalo robe of commerce was probably looked upon by the outer world as the animal's final cause; but in the North-West the robe was of secondary importance. The leather, the raw hide and sinews were of the highest value to all classes of the people, and were such conveniences that even now they are greatly missed by all who have been accustomed to their use. The robe was not so much a necessity as the source of the plain Indian's or the plain hunter's luxuries—his trinkets, his finery, his sugar, tobacco and rum—though the latter was generally kept by the post trader to extort provisions from him, when they happened to be scarce.

The buffalo's coat was in the best condition in mid-winter. In spring the hair lost its beautiful gloss, and became loose. The preparation of robes for export and of buffalo leather prepared like the moose-skin, for home use, was the Indian women's most laborious work ; and when one thinks of the enormous quantity of both which came from their hands, one is lost in wonder at such slavish and untiring labour. In making the robe the hide was first fleshed with a peculiar bone, notched like a comb, and then stretched on a frame to dry, after which it was wetted and again reduced with a scraper to the proper thickness. At this stage it was frequently split down the back, though this reduced the value of the robe, and then thoroughly dried over the lodge fires. It was now greased and allowed to hang for several days when it was again wetted on the flesh side until quite soft, after which the brain and liver of the buffalo, mixed in a paste, were vigorously rubbed into the hide, which was again dried. The final process was the most laborious of all. A stout pole was planted in the lodge and a cord of sinew twisted like a bow-string attached to its top and bottom, yet loosely, so as to admit the hide, fold after fold of which was then, for a long period, hauled back and forth against the rough string until the whole inner pelt was thoroughly softened. When this process was completed the hide became a marketable robe. A fluffy or wool-like surface was given to the pelt afterwards, by rubbing it with a boss-bone or rough stone ; and such robes, prepared by the Indians for their own use, were frequently adorned with pictures painted in bright colours, and not without spirit.

The leather, though sometimes exported, was generally reserved for home use, and contributed largely to domestic comfort. Out of it the plain Indian made his moccasins and other articles of clothing, his saddles, and above all his portable and comfortable lodge, for comfortable it was in winter, with its lining and carpeting of soft buffalo robes, and its bright fire, round which the legends of the tribe were handed down to the youngsters in the long winter nights. Indeed the buffalo skin lodge was in general use twenty years ago even in the settlements, and was often preferred in summer to the house. The same style of lodge is still in use in the North-West; but it is now made of calico instead of leather. On the plains, the buffalo dung, called "buffalo chips" by the hunters furnished, in summer, the Indian and plain-hunter's fuel, and its sinews, which lay immediately under the back-fat, along the spine from the sirloin forward, supplied tough and durable thread and glue. The last, but not the least, important product of the buffalo was shaganappi, or as it was often called "North-West Iron." The word in common use is a corruption of the Cree compound pesaganappi ("shred in a circle"), and the common sort was simply a long strip cut concentrically from the hide of an old bull. But the twisted lines, which were used for bridle lines, tethers, etc., were taken from the rump of the animal. where the hide was uniform in thickness. These lines, like the others, were cut from the hide in continuous concentric rings, which were afterwards greased and exposed to the sun, pounded to suppleness with a mallet, or better still, chewed, and then braided. They were exceedingly strong and durable. Shaganappi was in fact, until recently, an invaluable and omnipresent article in the North-West. It was much stronger and more durable than the cordage made from domestic hide, and was largely employed in making cart and double harness for cattle. For lashing there was nothing equal to it. First wetted, and then warped around a broken wheel, or shaft, it contracted in drying, to a grip as firm as iron ; and indeed, as has been said, this is the name it often went by.

Such were the principal benefits which the buffalo conferred upon the Indians, half-breeds and old settlers of the North-West, and which covered most of their primary needs. It seems but yesterday when they were in the full enjoyment of them ; and it is not surprising, therefore, that a generation "to the manner born" should look back with regret to the past and heave many a sigh at thought of its primitive happiness and abundance. So strong is this feeling that I verily believe if to-day such a miracle could happen as the sudden appearance of an immense bison herd between the two Saskatchewans the reaper would be left in the swath, and the ripened grain would cry in vain for harvesters.

In this paper, which has grown to greater length than I intended, there is not space to describe the known attempts which have been made since European settlement began on the continent to domesticate the buffalo, and to cross it with domestic cattle. Various mention is made of such efforts in the last century, but necessity did not compel the early colonizers to subdue the animal to their use, and hence the experiment was never seriously tried upon a large scale. It has certainly been broken to harness, and I remember that a buffalo at Edmonton was spoken of twenty-two years ago as a trained animal. But the strong argument in favour of preserving the buffalo does not lie in this direction, but in its possible value in cross-breeding. There are enormous districts in the high latitudes of the North-West which will yet be of great productive value if a hybrid animal can be developed hardy enough to endure the winter. It is therefore of importance that an effort should be made to preserve the animal in order that the question may be settled by systematic experiment. This has been tried to a limited extent by private enterprise, as for example at Stony Mountain and Silver Heights in Manitoba, and at Prince Albert on the Saskatchewan. But the recent dispersion of the Stony Mountain herd proves that such experiments should be the care of the government, and be given a much wider application than has yet been attempted. Doubts used to be expressed whether the buffalo would cross with domestic cattle, and even General Marcy, a man of large experience on the American frontier, was firmly of opinion that they would not. He based his opinion upon the statement of a trader among the Chickasaws who herded forty buffaloes with domestic cattle, yet never knew them to cross.

Be this as it may, we know that in the North-West the animals cross freely, and their offspring have been seen by hundreds of people in Manitoba and on the Saskatchewan. The fact of successful cross-breeding, and of the fertility of the three-quarter crossed cow, is now beyond dispute, and it only remains to determine the best method of preserving the buffalo itself from extinction, for without this the hybrid strain would ultimately die out. The first point to settle, with a view to experiment, is locality, which of course should be both safe and suitable. The prairie instantly suggests itself, since the bison is a prairie animal ; and if the experiment could be safely carried out there, it would undoubtedly be the best locality. But on the prairie it would be difficult to prevent the animal from roaming, and so becoming the prey of the pot-hunter, as was the case with the estrays from Stony Mountain. As settlements multiplied around them they would prove troublesome to farmers, who, being quite satisfied with their "short horns," and caring nothing for high latitude stock raising, would probably show them but scant courtesy. We must look farther west. The foot-hills of the Rocky Mountains, and even beyond them, were favourite ranges of the buffalo in times past, and, in view of this, western Alberta is perhaps a more promising place for the experiment than any other. If the animals were confined they would probably become sterile, and the experiment fail, but if a special national park were set aside for the purpose they might be protected, and yet enjoy comparative freedom, and thus have a chance of survival. If the experiment upon fair trial proved successful it would then be taken up elsewhere, and would lead to important results. In the meantime an effort might be made to introduce the bison in other regions. In a great grazing country, with vast vacant areas like West Australia, it would probably thrive and multiply, and the experiment might easily be tried there. No reasonable effort should be spared to rescue an animal from destruction which has been of great service on our continent, which is intimately associated with its history, and whose extinction would be a disgrace to civilized man.

———————

Note.

In treating of the diminutive variety of the prairie bison, called by some Amiskoo-sepe-moostoos, and which I scarcely think has before been described, I set down what appeared to me to be the most obvious origin of the name. But at the same time I should have given another name which the animal bore, whose derivation, however fanciful it may appear, has yet its strong supporters among native hunters, both Indian and half-breed. Not long ago I met with a statement in print that the bison never roamed the Pacific slopes. This, of course, is a misstatement ; and, though I did not say so in my article, I am yet of opinion that the singular variety referred to, called by some Amiskoo-sepe-moostoos, or Beaver River buffalo, and by others Amiskoo-sip, or beaver duck buffalo was the animal peculiar to the regions west of the Rocky Mountains, north of the Columbia River. Among others, that fine old Cree chief Attakacoop (Star-Blanket) has assured me that many years ago he saw this variety of the bison in great abundance beyond the western slopes of the mountains. It is not improbable, therefore, that this breed came originally from the west, having forced its way over the mountains to the plains of the interior, where it retained its marked physical characteristics to the last. The term Amiskoo-sip-moostoos, or beaver duck buffalo, illustrates the propensity of the Indians towards a fanciful nomenclature. Amiskoo-sip is the name given by the Crees to a shy little duck of the merganser family, which in the North-West is usually found in the neighbourhood of beaver dams and in the ponds made by these animals. By a loose analogy the Indians applied the term to the diminutive buffalo of the prairie.

When referring to the young buffalo bulls and cows I should have mentioned that, unlike domestic cattle, they did not rut until their fourth or fifth summer, nature severely punishing the bulls for any transgression of her rule in this respect. It was after that age that the latter began to sharpen their horns. The flat surfaces worn upon the outer bend of all full-grown buffalo horns must not be confounded with this sharpening process. These surfaces were due to wallow-making, the hole or depression in the soil being first formed by a vigorous use of hoof and horn. These depressions could not be made in the prairie in the North-West in winter, and therefore the animal simply rolled in the snow during that season. True wallowing took place in spring, when the animal's coat began to loosen, that is to say towards the end of May, and then its wallowing was undoubtedly intended to facilitate the process of shedding. Wallowing had the curious effect of not only matting, but of actually felting, the coat, so that it fell off in large thick sheets, which looked exactly like pieces of brown blanket. When lifted from the buffalo's sides by the wind these flaps gave the animal a most grotesque appearance, and, when dropt, were made use of by the Indians for comfortables, caps, and even saddle-cloths. This fact no doubt gave rise to Morton's statement in his " New English Canaan," published in 1637, that the Indians manufactured the buffalo's wool into cloth. In my article I omitted referring to several oft-described methods employed by the Indians in the capture of the buffalo, amongst others the " pound." Calves, cows and bulls were indiscriminately butchered when caught in this way, a fact which seems to conflict with the statement that the Indian hunter received severe punishment for wanton slaughter. The explanation is that the killing of every empounded beast was due to a deeply rooted superstition. It was believed that if a single animal escaped there would be an end of pound-making. A like superstition seems to prevent the Indians in the North-West from bringing in a moose or red deer head with the neck-skin attached. It is difficult to induce even christianized Indians to do so. Pound-making, too, was intended to supply the helpless and needy in a great camp with the necessaries of life. For obvious reasons it has entirely ceased among our Indians; but it is still an Asiatic custom, and is made use of to this day in the sultanry of Pahang, in the capture of the gaur, or East Indian bison.

www.ingramcontent.com/pod-product-compliance
Lightning Source LLC
Chambersburg PA
CBHW080822280726

48660CB00018B/3570